MAGNIFY

PURPOSE

An Introvert's Guide to
Creating a Coaching Business
that Reflects Who You Are

Stacey Weckstein

NEW YORK

LONDON • NASHVILLE • MELBOURNE • VANCOUVER

MAGNIFY YOUR PURPOSE

© 2018 Stacey Weckstein

Published in New York, New York, by Morgan James Publishing in partnership with Difference Press.
www.MorganJamesPublishing.com

The Morgan James Speakers Group can bring authors to your live event. For more information or to book an event visit The Morgan James Speakers Group at www.TheMorganJamesSpeakersGroup.com.

ISBN 978-1-68350-665-2 paperback
ISBN 978-1-68350-666-9 eBook
Library of Congress Control Number: 2017910828

Cover Layout & Interior Design by:
Megan Whitney
Creative Ninja Designs
megan@creativeninjadesigns.com

In an effort to support local communities, raise awareness and funds, Morgan James Publishing donates a percentage of all book sales for the life of each book to Habitat for Humanity Peninsula and Greater Williamsburg.

Get involved today! Visit
www.MorganJamesBuilds.com

This book is created by source, coming divinely through me and my gifts in this lifetime.

I am humbled and honored to travel each journey with my clients. They trust me in a way that allows them to get to the vulnerable parts of who they are in order to achieve their deepest desires and biggest passions. They truly demonstrate that you can have anything you set your mind to.

CONTENTS

VI • Magnify Your Purpose

FOREWORD

The coaching profession is both a noble and a heart-centered pursuit. Many coaches find their way into the industry out of a love for other people and a desire to serve, and I find it incredibly heartening to see how the career of coaching is booming as an industry.

However, I've also read some troubling statistics, like how most professional coaches earn less than $10,000 a YEAR as a coach. So it makes you wonder, what's happening? If there is such a need for coaches in the world, and if these coaches loves to serve people, why aren't they making money from their coaching?

In my 25 years of training Health Coaches as the founder and director of the Institute for Integrative

Nutrition, what I've discovered is this: The same traits that make someone an excellent coach are generally the same traits that hold them back.

Their ability to be quiet, take a back seat, and listen is what keeps them shy and in the corner. What makes them keen and attentive to another's person's problems are what keep them from wanting to speak up and offer their services at a price.

In "Magnify Your Purpose", Stacey makes a case for how each entrepreneur deserves a profit for following their passion, as well as how to take the traits that make you an excellent coach and repurpose those same traits to allow you to become an excellent business owner.

At Integrative Nutrition, we teach the concept of bio-individuality in nutrition there's no one diet that works for everyone. And what I see Stacey do so brilliantly here is apply that same concept to running a business – creating a business that's so uniquely you, rather than one that fits the traditional mold.

If you've been struggling to make your coaching practice a success, if you've felt that your gifts in some ways hold you back, I implore you to keep reading this book. In the pages, you'll not only find companionship, but also an experienced explanation of how you can reverse your situation to become a highly successful and confident coach and business owner.

Joshua Rosenthal
Founder and Director, Integrative Nutrition

INTRODUCTION

"What do you want to be when you grow up?" It's the question we all hear, starting from a very young age. I never had an answer and now I know why: I have always been a gal who made it up as I went along.

All my life, I've gravitated toward the things that interested me, even if they didn't make any sense in the context of future goals. Along the way, I had a lot of doubt about how I was going to make a career out of my work experience, the subjects I had studied, and the things I love to do.

But by age 33, all the pieces of my puzzle finally came together and made sense. It turned out that my seemingly unrelated passions, interests, and areas of expertise were the perfect combination I needed to build my coaching practice and work with my clients. Who would have thought that a background in psychology, culinary arts, retail management, holistic health coaching, and energy work would ever make sense together in a business? It was a moment of sheer bliss when I realized I could create a career and help people just by sharing the things I love to do.

When I figured out how to make all my talents relevant, to use them to tell a compelling story in order to create services I could offer my clients, not only did my career begin to feel deeply satisfying, it also attracted the type of clients who could really benefit from what I had to offer. I began operating my business from a place of knowing myself, and of bringing all my passions and purpose into one place to be of service to others.

Once I put this all together, the next thing I did was freak out. Because I knew I actually had to start *doing those things*, and I had no confidence in or ways of expressing myself that I thought would capture the attention of people who really needed me. I was really shy about talking to people I didn't know and trying to find something in common. The idea of starting a conversation with someone new or going to a networking event to try to "get clients" scared me so much it had me second-guessing the idea of creating and marketing my own business.

But I figured it out and that's why I'm writing this book. I learned how to do what I love in a voice that confidently portrays who I am and what I have to offer. You can, too.

For me, as an introvert, the hardest part of bringing my creativity and my message to prospective clients was learning how to engage others and start talking about what I had to offer the world. At first, I was so timid that I only discussed my passions with the people who were closest to me – my family. The problem with that was that although they loved that I had varied interests, they didn't believe my skills and passions were traditional enough to take out into the world and combine to make a career.

Watch Stacey and see what strange thing she comes up with next! There was no place for unique thinking in the small community I had set up for myself, so I felt

I had no choice other than to find my voice, figure out how to make it feel compelling, get my butt out of the house, and connect with new people.

Speaking in public was an issue my whole life. I have this very distinct memory of my fifth-grade science class, where I was assigned a project that I would then have to present to the room. As it came time for my turn I could feel all the butterflies in my tummy spreading all over my body, and I wanted to throw up. The fear that my classmates would be bored or tease me about my presentation was so overwhelming that when I went to the front of the room I literally forgot my own name. Now I had proven my fears right! As a result, there were years when I wouldn't do a live presentation without notes to read so I could look down and forget that anyone was watching me. That has since changed.

Fast forward to age 33, the year that everything changed for me. I was working then at Whole Foods Market, and talking to a friend about a cooking class I had just taken. I was so excited to share what I had learned about how to prepare raw foods! The store's marketing director overheard my conversation and asked me if I would like to teach a regular class in the café on a monthly basis. The sheer terror I felt left me frozen like a deer in the headlights. But then something happened that was so unexpected, I thought I was dreaming. I said, "Yes, I would love to do that!" As if something took over my brain and answered the question for me.

Of course, I went into panic mode for the two weeks between agreeing to do this terrifying thing and the actual class itself. I over-prepared, I practiced at home, and I made copious amounts of notes just in case I blanked. I even put my name at the top of the page!

On the day of the class, I was in the cafe setting up and a woman named Amy approached me and let me know how excited she was that I was teaching this class. I thanked her and blurted out, "I just hope I can remember my name, I have never taught a class before." She reassured me by telling me she was going to sit in the front row and that I should teach the class to just her.

As I started the class, I felt clumsy for the first five minutes, but as I started making the food and sharing samples, I fell into a flow. I was sharing what I knew, people were enjoying it, and I was expressing myself in a way that felt like me. I wasn't in science class anymore – I was talking to my best friend Amy as if we were at lunch. I was simply sharing my new favorite smoothie recipe with her, and she was very excited to try it.

That day changed me forever. I have not been nervous since when talking in front of a group of people, because I had truly felt myself in my passion and got clear that the information and the message was no longer about me. It was about the information people had to have, and how I could share that to benefit their lives the way it had benefitted mine.

I'm writing this book for you; to help you fully excavate out your passion, make sense of it, and find your voice in your coaching practice and in the message you want to express. I want you to be able to get out into the world and connect with others in a way that keeps your passions and offerings feeling fresh without you feeling intimidated.

We often take what matters to us most and keep it to ourselves because we're shy, scared, or unsure.

We keep ourselves and our message small, because it feels overwhelming to go big. I am here to tell you that people want what you're offering – in fact, they need it. I found this out the slow, agonizing way, but you don't have to follow that path. I want to teach you a different path, the one that brings you out of your shell in the best, most comfortable way, a way that will leave you with no doubt that you are doing the work you are called to do. If you follow this guide as presented, you too will magnify your purpose and build the business that truly reflects who you are.

CHAPTER 1
Turning Passion Into Possibility

"If you are always trying to be normal, you will never know how amazing you can be."

MAYA ANGELOU

Finding your passion and realizing it is your career purpose in life is an exhilarating feeling. It is like a breath of fresh air filling up every cell in your body. You have renewed interest and energy to re-create your life and discover more meaning in what you do every day. It's that moment of bliss and delight that comes *before* you can even ask yourself, "How?"

and allow self-doubt to come rushing in. As you will see from my client Rachel's story, acknowledging your passions is one thing; putting them into action and overcoming life's obstacles and other people's expectations is quite another. If you don't follow through, you deny yourself the opportunity to do the things you love.

Teenaged Rachel spent countless hours browsing fashion magazines and dreaming of how she would look in high-fashion outfits. She learned how to sew and modify the clothes in her closet to look more like the designer trends she loved so much. She dreamed that one day she would find her place in the fashion industry and build a career that would allow her to, not only wear the clothes she loved so much, but also to make her own contribution to the fashion world.

But it didn't work out that way. The youngest of three girls whose immigrant parents had done well for themselves, Rachel had grown up with privilege, private schooling, and the advantages money could provide. With these advantages, however, came the expectation that Rachel and her sisters would go to college and choose a "proper" professional career rather than studying something creative that might not be as lucrative.

Rachel was expected to study the "right" things, marry a man who would be a good provider for the family, have a few children, and generally fulfill her family's very traditional expectations, all intended to keep her safe and secure. Since Rachel respected her parents and wanted to please them, she made what seemed like the "right" choice: she gave up on her dream of a fashion career and majored in journalism. She told herself it was okay. This way, she could be somewhat creative without taking on the risk of doing what she really wanted to do, which sounded crazy: dress people for a living.

But this denial of her passions led Rachel down a few dark paths in college; she never felt like she fully fit in anywhere. While her sisters got married and started their families, she felt stalled by failure and dashed expectations. Even meeting and marrying Jack, a kind, hardworking, religious man who wanted to have kids right away, didn't "fix" things. Why wasn't she feeling completely satisfied? She ignored this question that lightly tugged on her, determined to keep everyone else's dream for her intact.

Rachel loved being pregnant. She would find ways to dress herself in the styles she loved. When she dressed herself and her belly, she felt like the women in the magazines she adored. She adorned herself in accessories and styled her clothes in such ways that either concealed or revealed her baby bump, depending on what she wanted that day. She loved playing dress up with herself and her changing body. She was a highly fashionable pregnant woman, and her friends took notice, telling her that they, too, wanted to look put-together and stylish while pregnant.

Rachel started giving fashion advice and going shopping with friends, helping them find maternity clothes that looked like the everyday outfits they normally would wear, instead of the oversized and unflattering tents they'd been settling for. Then she'd go back to her friends' houses and end up clearing space in their closets by explaining what was no longer in style and creating fresh, more contemporary outfits with what they already had.

When Rachel dressed her friends, she felt nourished by the experience. She loved not only how her friends looked in their new clothes, but also how they felt like their best selves when the clothes fit so well and highlighted their personalities. Helping her friends in this way reignited her passion for fashion and allowed her to be home with her two young boys.

She knew that staying in the life she'd created from making the "right" choices would continue to feel uninspired, and that she'd just be going through the motions to meet other people's expectations. But she couldn't figure out how to make money doing what she loved. Here she was, a creative professional and a budding fashion coach, and she didn't know how to ask to get paid. How would she be able to explain her services and what she represented in a compelling way without coming across as pushy and scaring people off?

Like many new coaches, Rachel hid, at first, behind a blog she'd started for fun. She would highlight the fashion trends she was interested in, write about how the reader could save money putting the look together, and then invite them to hire her for help. But because the only people who read her blog were family and friends, she didn't get paying clients.

Writing came easily, but the idea of getting out of the house and soliciting strangers to talk to about fashion was harrowing. How could she talk in front of groups of people? Did she have anything to say? Why would anyone take her seriously? Sure, she had experience dressing her friends – but they were her friends and they knew and trusted her. She felt selfish and guilty for wanting to follow her passion. Those feelings and insecurities got in the way of her bringing her passion for fashion out into the world and offering her expertise and services to those who would benefit greatly.

Another obstacle was that Rachel, like many of us, was taught that business is conducted in one specific way, a series of policies and procedures that need to be precisely followed in order to be successful. But Rachel, also like many of us, is a creative; she isn't her most productive inside a traditional and inflexible structure. Rachel had a short attention span, and she also needed to divide that scattered attention between many things, including being a stay-at-home mom. How was she ever going to make this work?

Many coaches and creative professionals find their passion careers later in life, when they are no longer able to ignore their calling. Because these passions aren't commonly taught in a college setting, many don't know that building a creative business is even an option. The traditional world doesn't teach that you can create a business out of your hobbies. Instead, we're taught that we must follow specific steps, in specific ways, and under specific circumstances in order to be successful, make money, and live a comfortable life.

This just isn't true. There are ways to figure out your own working style so you can be the most productive version of yourself in your business. There is a business you can put together from all the things you love to do: a business that will make sense and be of benefit to others. Many new coaches start off their practices thinking they have to do things in a particular way, and often do not see that their other interests and passions can be a part of their businesses. Your puzzle pieces, just like mine, do fit together when you find the connecting thread that tells the story of how they all work together. The trick is finding that story and connecting all the dots in a way that makes sense to you – and then it will make sense to your clients too.

There are so many professionals, like Rachel, who followed the career path they thought they should for reasons of false security. And there are so many parents that pressure their kids onto a specific path because they just want the best for them. It's really not your fault that you didn't know there were other options and other, less traditional, ways of doing business and being of service to others. Even if there'd been an instruction manual somewhere on making a career out of doing what you love when it doesn't fit a traditional business model, there still wasn't a 101-level class at school.

Now that you understand why following your passion pays off, the next question becomes, "Where do I start?" The short answer is: with yourself! The process of starting a new business or coaching practice in any industry is tough. New coaches must take an inventory of their interests and life experiences to figure out how they will coach, who they want to work with, and on which topics. The process of starting a business that really speaks to who you are and how you want to work with others starts to bring up your patterns and self-doubt that will have you blocking yourself in so many ways that you will think these are legitimate reasons not to forge ahead. You may be reading this book because you have already started this process and you are stuck somewhere trying to figure out how to bring yourself and your creation into the world. There are so many places to hide in the process of reconfiguring ourselves and building our creative business! If you can cultivate the awareness that all that is simply resistance and keep moving along and observing what comes up in every step, it may be a smoother journey.

At this point you may be asking yourself, "What makes Stacey Weckstein (or however you pronounce her name) an expert in any of this?" Sometimes I ask myself the same question – that's one of the places my insecurities come up. The definition of expert is a person who has a comprehensive and authoritative knowledge of or skill in a particular area. What makes *me* an expert is having been through this process on which you are embarking. I understand how you feel. I know the places where you could potentially block yourself technically or emotionally, and I know how to guide you to the other side without getting stuck in all the places I did. By reading this book, you are allowing me to fulfill my full potential and passion in being a teacher and guide. In turn, I am supporting you as you learn to understand yourself better, gain the confidence to come into who you are, and serve others as the expert *you* are meant to be. It is truly my pleasure to be of service to you in this way, and I am deeply honored to have paved the way, every bump and heavy brick, to make this journey smoother for you.

CHAPTER 2
Possibility Into Purpose

"Soul work is not a high road. It's a deep
fall into an unforgiving darkness that
won't let you go until you find the song
that sings you home."

McCall Erickson

There are no coincidences, only synchronicities that
do not always make sense until the story has fully
revealed itself. I offer my story as an example of how
life purpose can come together and make sense once
you can identify the answers to a few key questions.

As I was growing up, there were lots of different sports, arts and crafts, music, and religious studies available to me. I would bounce around from one thing to the next, feeling excited about each new activity, until I quickly moved on to the next thing that caught my interest. It was fun to try new things, and to feel my body and mind used in different ways. But once I figured out the strategy behind the new interest, I would start to become bored because I felt I had mastered the activity. Mastery, in my mind, was gaining full understanding – as opposed to practicing it for long amounts of time to reach a certain degree of proficiency. My plan was to collect skills: as many as interested me.

There's a saying: "Jack of all trades, master of none." That was definitely me and I liked it that way. But my process of collecting skills and tools was seen to the outside world as the inability to commit and stick with one thing long enough to become a master. Instead of seeing my process for the creative exploration it was, I began to see it as a character flaw. I felt ashamed and forced myself to sit through things in boredom in order to prove to my parents that I could stay with something. It didn't last. I realize now (and teach my clients) that there is no shame in having many tools. In fact, it's a huge asset, this ability to combine many skills, interests, and trades into the perfect, personalized, right-fit business.

I pride myself on accomplishing tasks quickly. I do not feel I have to have them perfectly done, and most the time I won't go back and correct my mistakes. My college experience reflected this, as I zoomed through all the boring required courses in order to finally decide on a major that I would love, psychology. I had been in therapy since I was five. My mother thought I needed someone to talk to after my parent's divorce. The therapist taught me how to take my feelings and put them into words. When I spoke my feelings, the tightness and butterflies in my body would flutter out, and I could relax.

As with the extracurricular activities I did when I was young, I wanted to quickly understand psychology and the way that it worked, and then put it in my toolbox. I minored in mythology, because it interested me and because, like psychology, all the stories had meanings that explained the archetypes of life. It actually made no sense to keep taking mythology courses, but the teacher was truly insightful in a way that kept me interested and looking for the hidden meanings in what people said and what I read.

The theme for me in all things that I chose to do was to look behind what was going on in front of my face. It was like an intriguing puzzle to be solved. Of course, at the time I had no idea this is what I was doing. I just knew that I liked what I chose to do and it held my interest. When it didn't anymore, I would be on to the next thing.

When I graduated with my BS in psychology, I had no interest in studying further, but the opportunities in my field without going on to graduate school were very limited. I felt hopeless; I was supposed to graduate with a great job on tap and high earning potential. Yet here I was. No other career path presented itself, so off I went to the campus career center for a counselor to help me sort my confusion and choose a new path.

The career center had many diagnostic tools to assess my personality and my abilities. The tests revealed that I was good with my hands and should consider the two top career choices at that point: hair stylist or chef. The problem with traditional career assessment is that it's too straight forward. Here's your skillset; here are the one or two jobs you can do with that skillset. It doesn't take into account creative jobs or how you can fuse your skillsets together to encompass everything you know how to do and also what you love.

Although I was very skilled at dyeing my own hair, I had a true passion for food. I loved textures and flavors of all kinds, and I enjoyed cooking. My mom would only cook things she could make in the microwave or toaster oven, and my grandmother didn't have the correct recipe card to boil water without burning the kettle. So cooking wasn't in my genes. However, my stepmother, who helped raise me from age five, is an amazing cook. She enjoys cooking and trying new recipes; it's one of the ways she shows love and care for her family. My stepmother and I love to talk about food, diets, and restaurants; when I went to college she gave me her arsenal of all my favorite recipes she made while I was growing up. I would throw dinner parties for my friends in my off-campus apartment just to try out recipes and have a reason to cook for more than one.

The day I visited Johnson and Wales University culinary school was one of the most sensational days of my life. Peeking in the windows of the classes and watching the chef instructor teach and walk around to assist at every student station, I instantly knew where my life was headed next. I started culinary school the following fall, and it was one of the best years of my life. But I wondered what I would do with my culinary degree. I couldn't see resigning myself to a kitchen and cooking for the rest of my life, no matter how much I loved food. I learned that the industry itself made it difficult to make a sustainable living and gain a good reputation. I worried about the hours of wear and tear on my body.

I decided to head out west to San Francisco and see what unfolded. The first opportunity that presented itself to me was with a well-known raw food chef. At the time, he was writing his first cookbook. My friend was a waitress at his restaurant and introduced me. I got the job immediately as a prep chef. At the time I had no idea what raw food was or how beneficial the lifestyle was to overall health and wellness. The dishes we prepared were uniquely creative and healthy, with wonderful, bold flavors that weren't quite like anything I'd learned in culinary school. Ironically, I still ate a burger for lunch at the place across the street.

During this period, I had the opportunity to standardize the chef's recipes, train the staff on policy and procedure, and clean up operations in general. Streamlining the processes for efficiency made me feel like I was creating the strategy of the business, and the chef was so impressed he asked me to do his bookkeeping next. But that wasn't something I felt qualified to or interested in doing, so I moved on.

Starbucks immediately hired me into management based on my previous experience, and I worked both preparing drinks and streamlining company policies and procedures. I was good at it. So good, in fact, that Starbucks created a position just for me; I was sent to several stores to clean up and retrain the staff. I loved feeling that my talents were truly seen and that my skills were well-used. After a couple years, I left the food service industry to become a stay at home mom. And thus begins the story of how I came to be a health and wellness coach.

During my first pregnancy, I developed gestational diabetes, which I was told could be controlled with diet and would go away as soon as the baby was born. After all my culinary experience, the thought of changing and monitoring my diet was horrifying. Food was one of the things I loved most in the world, and I had no desire to hold myself back from the foods I loved. Food was the way I connected with people and shared experiences!

I felt betrayed by my body, but once I got past the anger and put the food plan into place, I started to notice the changes and feel better. I was still counting the days until Ella was born so that I could have a huge bowl of pasta from my favorite restaurant across the street from the hospital where I was going to give birth. I had it all planned out. My life still revolved around food, it just had to revolve around different foods for a few more weeks – or so I thought.

Soon after my baby girl was born, I started to feel really awful. I developed a rash around my shoulders, back, and arms; my hair was falling out in clumps. I was exhausted all the time, really depressed, and my breast milk never came in. I went to my family doctor, but my blood work came back fine. How could I feel so lousy and have nothing be wrong? I chalked it up to postpartum readjustment and asked the women in my moms' group if they were feeling the same way. One of the moms told me about functional medicine. I had never heard of it, but I wanted to give it a try, considering how terrible I felt.

The doctor looked at my lab results, diagnosed me as hypothyroid, and gave me an eating plan, supplements, and some recommended lifestyle changes. My heart sank. I had a flashback to my mom's diet in the 1980s; she ate cardboard-dry chicken with lentils and rice for what seemed to be every meal. I used to tease my mother that she didn't need to worry about her health because the 75 or more vitamins she had to take every day were going to choke her to death. Now here I was, taking *my* 75 vitamins a day. Talk about karma!

On my doctor's recommendation, I removed gluten, dairy, and refined sugar from my diet. Fortunately, I found a wealth of recipes that actually tasted good and just needed to be prepared with alternative ingredients for my body to accept it and turn the nutrients into healthy cells. As a trained chef, I was fascinated by making healthy food taste good. I pledged to practice this diligently, now that I had to eat in a very specific way.

A few years, a move to Florida, and a second daughter later, I went back to work. I found an opportunity in the kitchen at Whole Foods Market and spent every day cooking healthy recipes that tasted great. Six months after I started, I was asked to join the Whole Body Team, and my life became very exciting. I was in charge of ordering and maintaining the health books. This gave me an opportunity to read everything on the shelf and learn about all the ingredients in food as well as vitamins so I could knowledgeably talk to customers about their product and lifestyle choices. I had an amazing team leader who put so much trust in me and was excited to teach me everything she knew. This job was my first glimpse into how my food, healthy lifestyle, and studies could be put to good use and help others. I felt inspired to go to work every day.

Raw foods made a return appearance in my life, and this time I finally read about and understood all the benefits. I bought recipe books and ate this way for three months. During this time, I found a weekend certification course to become a raw food chef. I was so fascinated with the lifestyle and how the chemistry of fresh organic uncooked food had the ability to heal the body. During this period, David Wolfe, a famous raw foodist, had a radio show. One day while I was listening to an interview of his, I heard him talk about a school where he was going to be speaking. I rewound the recording to catch the name of the school. As I listened to the rest of the show, I was already looking up the Institute for Integrative Nutrition.

As I read about the program, my body felt sparkly and effervescent. I had found something that spoke to my soul. A program where I could get certified to practice holistic health coaching and use my life's work and all the pieces on the path I had chosen, all in one profession. Suddenly my whole life made sense. I finally knew what I wanted to be when I grew up, a health coach. Everything I had been randomly doing based on my gut feelings and interests came together in one career story. My psychology degree would come in handy to get into some deep areas with clients around where they sabotage themselves. My love of food would take us into the kitchen to learn how to prepare foods that are quick, easy, and taste great, so that clients would have the tools to maintain their new lifestyle. I could also use everything I had ever learned about supplementation to help support their health and what they wanted to achieve. I felt of use and service to others by helping to support them in their health journey and finding their balance. And I could do it all based on my history and the interests I had learned and experienced my whole life.

For the first time, I didn't have to figure out what I should be doing in order to succeed. The answer was clear as day: make a career out of all the things I love to do and offer it in a way that brought in the things I've done my whole life that felt good and exciting. Even things I might do in the future could be incorporated into this new model I was creating for myself.

Until this time when my story came together in the form of a career choice, I never felt fully satisfied. I was pressured by society and family to find a traditional career or job. I never quite fit into any of the job descriptions available at companies. My talents went under-utilized and I would quickly get bored. Also my earning potential with a traditional company would quickly reach its limit. The idea of not being able to earn more, no matter how much work I put in, was upsetting and had me working under my capacity.

In the traditional working world, reward and recognition are not under our control. I hated this because being recognized by others in order to get a promotion or a raise was not always a matter of hard work or ingenuity, but rather someone else's experience of me. The work environment didn't feel like a place I truly belonged. I needed to create a space for myself where I could thrive regardless of someone else's opinion.

At first, this is a very scary venture, having to rely on your own self-love and hard work to succeed. This is where inner work really comes in. Self-approval, confidence, and drive take on a different perspective and dynamic when you work for yourself, and can be a source of motivation – or self-sabotage. Usually it is both. It is something I still struggle with every day, but now I have strategies and tools to keep me on track, which I will teach you.

I couldn't see it at the time I was participating in each piece of the puzzle, but synchronicity found a way for me to combine it all in service to others. After many years of learning how to have a creative business as a coach, I started to coach others on their creative talents and see how their bigger pictures, the ones that included all the things they loved, could fit into a business. I was able to help them fully step into what they love to do and create a message to attract clients who needed their support.

Consider your own life story...

Write down your own life story so that you can easily identify your patterns and go deeper into certain aspects of it. The pieces may not make sense until you look at them as a whole and then go through the rest of this book to learn how to create your new story.

If this feels overwhelming or confusing to you, start with your resume. Write out the things you liked to do and were good at in each of your jobs and schools. Think back to your childhood about which hobbies and interests you gravitated toward. Consider the types of things you find yourself interested in reading. This exercise will help you take stock of the things that really excite you and that you may want to share with others.

CHAPTER 3
Leveraging Your Life Story

"Maybe the journey isn't so much about becoming anything. Maybe it's about un-becoming everything that isn't really you so you can be who you were meant to be in the first place."

PAUL COELHO

Your life story can reveal so much about what you love to do and how you go about doing it. By taking a deeper look at how you interact with the world and identifying your patterns, you can start to formulate which aspects of yourself will really shine through in your business. By doing the exercises in this chapter around your passion, you will be surprised at how much skill you already possess to start your business. You will uncover the areas where you may need a few more tools and identify how to get them.

Coaching programs are a good place to learn basic skills to guide others. They also offer you the opportunity for self-discovery because as you go through the training, you learn lessons that are applicable to your own life and that can open you up to changing the areas that no longer serve you. Before I started training to be a coach, I remember feeling that, no matter how much I explained my insights on healthy living or energy work, the people in my life couldn't understand why I would be interested in such things. My social skills were minimal, and meeting new people felt like a daunting experience unless they introduced themselves to me first. Group classes or meetings were harrowing. I stayed close to the back wall and watched people talking to each other. On the rare occasion that someone came to talk to me and we made friends, I would attach myself to that person and follow them around the room to get an introduction to other people in an attempt to feel more comfortable. I was a classic introvert.

The first day at The Institute for Integrative Nutrition (IIN), the auditorium swarmed with 2,500 people all getting to know one another. I had met my mother's friend Kay during the summer. She was taking the course as well, and we met in front of the building before class so I would have someone familiar to sit with.

I made my way to my seat. Kay was on my right, for a sense of security, and on my left was a woman around my age, who introduced herself to me. We exchanged stories of why we were attracted to IIN and what we were doing in our lives with health and wellness. It was remarkable that our stories completely matched up. We both worked at Whole Foods Market, we both were into energy healing, we were both raw foodists, and we both followed David Wolfe.

It was the first time someone really heard me explain myself and didn't look at me as if I were speaking a language they didn't understand. In fact, as we discussed some of our shared areas of interests in depth, I felt seen, accepted, and understood. This was my tribe! This moment gave me permission to come out and finally start to navigate what it meant to be me, to step into this new career, and to feel this belonging every day. As time went on, I got more comfortable with approaching other people and not waiting for them to start the conversation. I was gaining confidence in who I was, and starting to understand who I was meant to be.

There are many ways to go about this process without signing up for an expensive program. A good place to start is by going over the story you wrote out in the last chapter, looking over your experiences, and picking the areas that really excited you. As you start to pick out the pieces of what you like to do, feel into your body. What sensations are you experiencing as you go through this journey and highlight for yourself where your interests lie? Here are some questions to consider and examples of how some of my clients became clear on what their creative passions are:

What things do you like to do that you find yourself excited by and interested in sharing with others?

As Jessica started to explore alternative therapies for her digestion, she realized she was fascinated with Nutrition Response Testing (NRT). How could testing the muscle response give so much accurate information about allergies and imbalances in the body? All she knew was that she was feeling better, and her digestion issues were clearing up. She took courses in NRT and practiced on her friends and family. She was in awe of the improvements she was seeing in their health issues as well. Jessica was so excited that even though she was normally quite shy, she couldn't help talking to everyone about what she was experiencing. She began to think this might be something she would want to do as a profession if she ever were to leave her current profession.

What is your work style? Identify ways in which you work best.

Amy loves to organize her life and found herself looking around her friend's homes and organizing their things in her head. Instead of browsing clothing magazines, Amy would find herself looking through the Container Store catalogue and thinking about how she could creatively purpose the storage containers that were being featured. When she started to offer her organizing service, Amy was working full-time and had no intention of leaving her non-profit education career. Her specific time blocks to work with clients were on the weekends and sometimes in the evenings after work for a follow-up mini clean-up session. Amy liked to build structure into her schedule so she knew where her time would be dedicated. Working non-business hours gave her the opportunity to keep her job and build a creative business that would bring in some extra income while doing what she loved.

Which past work skills or experiences excited you and made you feel of use?

I often have my clients look through their resumes and do a writing exercise describing their job duties and responsibilities. They then sort their daily, weekly, and monthly tasks into two columns: one for the things that they liked to do and that created flow in their day, and the other for skills they needed to use that didn't feel natural and caused them to feel negative about the job. Identifying the tasks and responsibilities that make you feel productive and of use in your career is where you will want to put your focus as you start to create the initial details of the business you'd like to do.

Which skills did you perform that you liked or disliked? Is there a common theme or thread to the jobs you've had in the past?

What topics did you enjoy studying?

This is also a written activity, one that goes back into your history to identify what types of clubs and classes you liked in school. What was it about the topic that interested you and that you find yourself sharing with others? What books do you tend to gravitate towards that you can add to the list of topics you'd like share with others?

How do you like to work with others?

For the first couple of years of her health coaching practice, Susan met her clients in her home office. She liked to meet her clients in person and do some cooking with them at each session. After some time, Susan had to move. Her new home was too small to have clients over without disturbing her husband, so she started seeing clients over Skype. Susan realized there was more flexibility in seeing clients this way and started planning for one, longer in-person cooking class towards the middle of the client's program. She also started to get more clients that did not live within driving distance, boosting her income. Although she had felt cozy cooking at home, the clear advantage of doing things differently had her reevaluating how she worked with clients.

What interests or hobbies do you like to be a part of or find yourself talking about?

Most of the stories in this book show how the interests, hobbies, and modalities that healed my clients' lives became their passions. For Rachel it was fashion, Amy liked organizing, and Danielle, Jessica, and Susan all healed themselves in some form of mind, body, or spirit way that then called them to heal others and support their life decisions.

Where are your friends asking you for help?

Your friends come to you for advice about something. They already think of you as an expert, that you are their go-to person for this thing. What is it? Could it be something you feel passionate or excited about that you could use to help more people?

Identifying what interests you and moves you, even if it is not a skill you have currently, will be helpful in starting this journey. As you answer these questions, are you getting a sense of specific patterns about yourself that you can use to maximize your productivity; to feed your excitement about working on something that really speaks to who you are?

All your answers to the above questions can weave together into a story that creates a framework for your passions. Your purpose will become working with others to support them with your services, or to help bring them out into their passion.

As I shared with you earlier, talking with a career counselor and taking some basic diagnostic tests can highlight your strengths and weaknesses, learning style, and suggested career paths. Shedding some light on the areas where you excel can only help to support your areas of interest.

To get a deeper, behind-the-scenes understanding of yourself and what your purpose is, you could have a reading with your local astrologer. Astrology is the study and influence of objects in the cosmos such as planets and stars. These astrological components impact our human lives. An astrology reading can help to clarify and articulate negative patterns and give you clear direction as to how to work with them, heal them, and take steps to begin to move beyond them.

When Danielle had her first astrology reading, she was at a place in her life when she knew she needed to make a change but talking with her therapist wasn't helping her move forward. She confided her frustration to a friend who recommended an astrology reading with the friend's astrologer, Anne, explaining the benefits she'd had from a reading and how the insights shared helped her get clear on her plans moving forward. Danielle loved to read her horoscope every day and see if her day panned out the way the local paper told her it would, but never heard of an astrology reading before. What could it hurt? She had no idea where to steer her life, and decision-making had become overwhelming. When she arrived at Anne's house for her reading, Danielle was greeted with an affable hello and a precise explanation of what she could expect from the 90-minute natal chart reading. Anne explained to her she could ask questions at any time, and this gave Danielle comfort.

Anne started to weave a story together of who Danielle was according to her birth chart. Danielle was impressed. She had never met Anne before, yet she was hearing things about herself only she knew to be true. She was delighted that someone could really see her deeper places that she was shy about bringing out to show others. Anne unearthed Danielle's interest in the occult and metaphysical arts and told her that she was going to find a way to teach these things to others. At that time, Danielle had just started taking an interest in these things and started to ask Anne questions about her studies. She felt comfortable with Anne because she felt Anne understood and held no judgment of her interests. Anne went as far to say that Danielle would soon be studying astrology as well, and that in the future she would use it with clients to help them see parts of themselves they needed to heal to move forward in life. Danielle felt so much permission to be herself and pursue her interests during this reading that she was ready to go home and start reading about basic astrology. When she left the session, Danielle felt so clear in the areas she hadn't been able to figure out for herself that her forward momentum in life reengaged.

Another way to see your purpose is to have a human design reading. Human design is the synthesis of Eastern and Western astrology, the Chinese I Ching, the Hindu chakra system, Kabbalah, and quantum physics. Similar to astrology, it uses your birth data, in this case entered into a computer program to generate your chart. The chart shows your strengths and weaknesses, your path and life purpose, what you are here to do and, most importantly, how to do it. It is a concrete strategic plan summarizing what is unique to you and what you need to do to manifest an amazing life.

Human design has less room for interpretation than astrology and is more strategy-based. It has a more scientific feel to it, as it directly pinpoints your personality, strategy, purpose, and flow style so you can make changes in the way you have been going about your life and using your energy for better flow and manifestation right away. My first human design reading was very basic, but the insights revealed and affirmed things I had suspected about myself. They showed me how to take action in order to get invited into the big things in life, such as career and relationships, with less friction and bitterness, better flow, and more lasting results.

My client Jessica was a successful photographer. She loved everything about her industry and she was financially supporting her lifestyle. But Jessica lived to work, and the long hours were starting to take a toll on her health. She wasn't eating regularly, and was out drinking and socializing five nights a week for her profession. Her digestion got so bad that she constantly had stomach cramps and blood in her stool and had started to miss work regularly. Jessica's friend Nancy called her to see how she was doing and they talked about the health issues. She referred Jessica to her doctor and warned it would be an unusual session, but she would start to see results right away.

Jessica immediately made an appointment. When she went the following week, the doctor told her he was going to communicate with her body through her muscles to see what was going on and what her body could not tolerate. He identified a list of foods and chemicals that were blocking Jessica's system – many of them were things Jessica was consuming on a regular basis. At the end of the session, the doctor gave her an easy-to-follow meal plan, some supplements, and small lifestyle changes. He would follow up with her regularly for six months to make sure she was healing, and they would modify her plan as time went on. As promised, Jessica started to improve right away. Over the next six months, she came to a place in her health she never thought possible. She felt great and wanted to tell everyone about her experience.

Jessica shared her story with Nancy. Nancy could hear the passion in Jessica's voice and told Jessica about the Institute for Integrative Nutrition (IIN). Nancy had attended the year before and had learned countless dietary theories as well as how to coach others and support them in a healthy lifestyle. Jessica knew she had to go. When she listened to the classes online, Jessica soaked up all the information and started to practice coaching other students in the program. She had no intention of quitting her day job. Now she had two careers she loved, and she would find a way to fit them both in. After earning her health coaching certificate Jessica decided it was time to learn and get trained in Nutrition Response Testing (NRT) as another health modality she could use with her clients. Having this diagnostic tool would be one more way she could help clients on a deeper level. Her weekend clients benefitted from her using these tools with them and then giving them ongoing support through her health coaching, just as her doctor had done with her. Over time, Jessica obtained the tools and training she needed to work with her clients. It had all started by simply identifying that she had a passion to share with others.

Everyone finds their answers in different ways. What is important is to remain open to discovering what it is you really love to do and to start to get more specific about how you love to do it. At this point, we can now fill in the pieces we'll need to paint the whole picture before going out into the world and offering it. For example, perhaps you need to further your education and take a training for some sort of license or certificate. Working on obtaining these missing pieces will fuel your passion and give you the clarity you need to feel confident to go onto the next steps of clearly speaking your message and attracting clients confidently.

CHAPTER 4
Find Your People, Find Yourself

"When you learn how much you're worth, you'll stop giving people discounts."

UNKNOWN

Once you are clear on all the tools you need and what you want to offer your clients, you are ready to get out and start sharing it. I know that for me, as an introvert, it can be hard to take my knowledge out into the world and tell others about it. It can feel vulnerable to take that place we hold so dear to our heart, the work we love so much and that has truly changed who we are, and share it with the outside world. There are going to be feelings of insecurity that will come up for you as you learn about yourself, start to identify who you want to work with, how to find them, and what to say. You may be tempted to reach outside yourself for confidence and approval, but what you'll really need to is to take these feelings and look to yourself for stability and clarity.

Before we head out the door, let's get clear on who you want to work with. This is called your target market. A target market (sometimes referred to as a niche market) is the group of people, statistically, that you see as your clients. This can be specified by many demographics of your choosing, including age, gender, earning potential, specific interests, and career path, to name a few. The more clear and specific you are about who you would like to work with, the easier it will be to find out where these people are. The biggest mistake that entrepreneurs make is to fail to decide on a target market. They end up looking everywhere for clients and not getting many, because it is difficult to talk about the benefits of your services when you aren't quite sure who you're talking to and what their problem is that you could solve. You certainly can be of service to anyone at any time, but having a focus can help your efforts be more precise and increase your sign-up rate.

Not everyone knows right out of the gate who they want to work with. I certainly didn't. The first year of my practice, I wanted to work with as many people as I could. I would talk to anyone who wanted to talk about health and wellness. I invited anyone who had a conversation with me about food, supplements, energy work, or cooking to a free session, which meant I gave away a lot of free sessions that didn't lead to a sign-up. The number one reason was that I had no way of identifying how I could be of benefit until after they agreed to work with me. Sure, there were people who just wanted to get healthy, and they felt confident in my knowledge and guidance. But it felt like pure luck when they signed on with me, as I hadn't really spoken to their problem or the benefits they would experience while working with me.

My first year, I worked with about 30 clients in one-on-one health programs. I probably gave away 200 free one-hour sessions. After this first year, I sat down and thought about each client, what I liked about working with them, and how I liked to work with them. I noticed my insecurities come up when we had the free sessions as well as the programs I did with clients that signed on. At the end of the year, I had identified that I enjoyed working with two distinct groups of people: female entrepreneurs who needed quick and easy ways to stay healthy on the go, and diabetics. I had identified these groups based on my experiences with my clients and where I felt the most useful. I'm going to take you through some things to think about so that you don't spend your first year floundering. Then you can maximize your conversion rate and avoid the burn-out I experienced by running around trying to talk to anyone who would listen.

Like Attracts Like

A good place to start is to take a look at the story you created when you were exploring what you like to do. Many creative professionals like to work with people who have similar needs, experiences, and backgrounds. You already understand where the client is in their journey and where they can end up, because you have conquered that thing they need help with.

Maybe there is a specific language associated with what you do, and the people you want to work with speak this language or want to learn it. For example, people who practice meditation or energy healing may discuss very specific ways they experience energy, and this may be expressed in specific terms that aren't used in everyday life or with "outsiders."

There are many people who can heal others and cannot heal themselves. They need you to support them while they do what they need to do to get to their goals. From this perspective, you can clearly see their problems, because at one point in time they may have been your problems, too. You can certainly speak more clearly to your own experience with those issues and assert with confidence that you know how to support these clients in getting what they want.

Opposites Attract

There may be people you don't have anything in common with, but what you are offering is still of benefit to them. This can be a tricky situation because you will be able to see where you can help them, but they may not be able to see it for themselves yet. You are not living your passion to force anyone to be a part of what you have to offer. Many new coaches feel they need to prove themselves to others by giving free advice, over-promising, or giving steep discounts or trades on their services just to get a client to say yes. This is never a good situation. If at any point you find yourself pushing someone into working with you or you are feeling challenged to "show them something" about your service before they have agreed to work with you, then this is probably not the person you are meant to work with and you should let them go. If you are compromising who you are, what you offer, or your worth, this is something to take a deep look at and to consider why you felt you needed to do that. You took this path because it makes you feel good, and the people you choose to work with should have you feeling good as well. Believe that your purpose and what you have to offer is of value to those who are meant to work with you.

For years, I offered health coaching at my acupuncturist's office. She would refer her clients to me to work on their food plans and help make their menus healthy and easy. One day, she referred both a dentist and a teenager to me for new client intakes. When the dentist walked in, I prejudged him to be smart and have an understanding of healthy eating and why it was so important. Apparently he felt he knew all there was to know about healthy eating and didn't feel he needed me, but he thought it would be interesting to hear what I was offering and how I felt I could best help him. We went through the questions of the introductory session, and instead of answering the questions in a way that would allow me to help him with his diet, he decided to question and challenge my motives and insights and press me for health information. When I got to the end of the session where I planned to explain how we could work together to reach his goals, we were both really defensive and combative. I was a new coach; the only thing I knew to do at the time was keep going through the session until the end, as painful as it was. What I should have done was stop the session and either explore with him why he felt he needed to give me a hard time (because maybe there was something emotional coming up for him that needed to surface and we could have continued), or I needed to end the session and let him know that I didn't feel we would be a good fit. Neither one of us walked away from that session feeling good or benefitted from the hour together.

My second session was with a 14-year-old girl who wanted to lose weight. I had prejudged her as well, thinking that a teenager would never eat healthy or comply. As we talked she told me about all the things she loved about junk food. I felt she would never give up her favorite foods. Her goal was to lose weight for high school, and when we came to the end of the session she was eager to sign on. Her mom made it clear that she would not be making any changes to the family diet, so her daughter would have to learn how to prepare all her own food for her new lifestyle.

As we worked together over the next six months, Ashley took her food and exercise seriously. We implemented small changes each session that she could practice and add into her lifestyle. She noticed how much better she felt without the candy. Even her friends were curious about her new foods, and started to bring healthier options to school too. By the end of the six months together, Ashley had not achieved her weight loss goal. As a new coach, I felt I had failed and I told her this. She told me she came in to lose 40 pounds and what she got was a lifetime of new good habits. She also knew where she had not stuck to her plan, and that maybe 40 pounds in six months was not a reasonable goal. The fact that she had learned so many new things she didn't know she would learn made her feel happy, and made me realize I had done a great job in supporting my client in getting what she wanted.

In both of these cases, self-worth issues came up for me to explore. I was looking to the dentist for acceptance and proof that I knew enough to work with him. In that session, I felt like I practically gave away my whole six-month program just to win his acceptance. I knew what I had to offer was amazing, and if I had just stayed in this knowing and been in acceptance of where he was in his journey instead of worrying about how I was coming across, that session would have gone very differently. We live and we learn.

It's valuable to understand your strengths and weaknesses. Again, you can refer to the self-history that you wrote when you were identifying what you wanted to do. There are things we are good at, and then there are places where we could use some help to focus on the things we are good at. For example, I am not good at keeping my financial books. The first year, I tried to do my finances myself, and it took up time I wanted to spend creating cooking classes and preparing for clients. I hired a part-time bookkeeper so I could make time for other things. It also made my taxes so much easier to put together at the end of the year! Can you identify places in your business where you can ask for help? Some areas that commonly need extra support are administrative duties, finances, technology, marketing, and follow-up. New coaches may need an accountability coach to talk with if they don't have a support system to make sure they are on track and thriving. It's tough when you have friends and family around you that are happy for your new journey but who can't really brainstorm with you or hold you accountable for accomplishments and staying on course.

They can also be your harshest critics. You have now become an innovator in your chosen area of expertise. You decided to leave your cookie cutter lifestyle to get ahead of the game in your new career. Some of the people in your inner circle are going to worry about whether it's smart to leave the comfort of a traditional career and a stable paycheck. Before you're solid and clear inside yourself that this is absolutely your path and that what you have to offer is your purpose, the people in your life will show up as that doubtful reflection of yourself to challenge you to grow your self-confidence around these changes you've decided to make. This is really important. Left unchecked, it leads to many coaches quitting after the first year because they don't have the support they need to keep moving forward and cultivating confidence.

Until you can clearly identify what you want, you are in a perpetual state of experimentation and elimination. This is perfectly normal for growth. The sooner you can get clear, the more focused your attention will be, and your efforts will result in a more streamlined and effective business.

CHAPTER 5
Creating Your Signature Message to Manifest Clients

"Shout-out to all the introverted, empathic, socially awkward souls who are pushing past their comfort zone to share gifts with the world."

ANONYMOUS

In the introduction of this book, I shared with you where my deep-seated fear of speaking came from. All it took was one embarrassing childhood experience for me to decide to shut my mouth publicly for the rest of my life. Just the idea of ever having to make a presentation or even talk in front of a group at a meeting or class made me feel so uncomfortable that I would hide in the back, take notes, and see the teacher after class if I had questions or comments. The shame of saying something incorrect or being made to feel wrong in front of a group felt like death.

When I trained to be a certified raw food chef, the class was structured to show us how to teach a class as we made each recipe. Because I had gone to culinary school, I was just taking this class out of interest and to learn how to make food in a different way than classical culinary cuisine. The fact that the teacher, Diana, was so passionate about the raw food lifestyle meant she believed in training her students to teach it forward and inspire their friends and loved ones. As a result, she got all her students excited to make raw food and share it with others, so they could feel the health benefits and claim the enthusiasm and ease of eating this way at home.

That's the effect she had on me, anyway. When I got home, I started telling all my coworkers at Whole Foods Market all about the things I had learned. I brought in raw food dishes every day for lunch and made extra to share. My team members were enjoying the food and word got to the marketing department that I was a certified chef and was making yummy raw foods.

In the introduction I shared with you how the marketing director approached me to teach a monthly raw food class and I knew I had to say yes. It was something that I benefitted from tremendously, and I loved to share the visceral experience with everyone by having them try the food and listen to my excitement about the subject.

I had forgotten for a minute that I was scared to death to talk in front of people when I agreed to teach this class. Then reality settled in, and I was frozen in sheer terror of what I had agreed to. I immediately started thinking of all the excuses I could make to cancel. When I calmed down, I realized I didn't want to back out. For the first time in my life, I wanted to figure out a solution through the problem.

What did I know to be true? I knew I was passionate and knowledgeable about the subject; I knew I was a great chef; I knew that the information and recipes I was going to share would be of great benefit to people who showed up at the class. And, honestly, if they didn't like the taste for whatever reason, I was totally okay with that. This realization gave me the confidence to start asking myself, "What is going to be the best way for me to give a presentation and make it feel as comfortable as I feel when I share this information with my coworkers, or my best friend at lunch?"

This revelation of how I wanted to feel in teaching my class led me to create my formula that I now use to train other coaches on how to teach a class based on what you love to talk about. I have seen many introverts and creative professionals use this formula and have such success with their level of comfort, their delivery of the message, the engagement of the audience, and the response of converting participants into clients.

To start this process, first I had to decide what I wanted to talk about. I had recently created a new smoothie recipe. I tested this recipe out on a few friends, and they loved it. So that was going to be my topic and the name of my class: *Creating a Smoothie You'll Want to Have Every Day*.

Once I identified the topic, I thought about the things I needed for my demonstration, like food and equipment. I made a list of these items so that I knew what to buy and what to bring with me on the day of the class.

Now for the tricky part: what I was going to teach while I made the smoothie. I decided to talk about the fact that I had originally created this recipe for my blood sugar issues. It was low in sugar, but had just enough sweet flavor to not taste "green" and bitter. I had researched the ingredients I added for highest nutritional benefit, and would share that information. And the last point I wanted to make was why I had chosen smoothies over juices.

A few days later, I was at lunch with a friend who is a fellow raw foodist. We were talking about the class I was putting together, and I told her about the smoothie and all the things that I was excited about. Out of that conversation came five good, key points as to why I was teaching this class. I took note of the topics I was enthusiastic about and that captured my friend's attention. There I had it: a five-point talk about the benefits of my smoothie that was engaging and informative. My audience was going to have a sensory experience of my smoothie by watching me make it, hearing me talk about the benefits, and tasting it for themselves. They would also go home with a handout of the recipe.

I was so excited that I'd found my unscripted content and that it felt so good to talk about. Just by having lunch with my friend, I created a whole speech of what I like to talk about in a way that was comfortable and exciting to my captive audience of one. Now, how could I make a lecture to more than 20 people and still feel like I was having a conversation with my girlfriend instead of feeling like I was talking at to a group? If I could just figure out this part, I thought, it would drastically reduce my anxiety over being the person at the front of the room all alone.

I thought the best way to do this would be to have a group discussion. I decided to poll the audience in the beginning with a couple of relevant questions that would tie into the topic of the class, by a show of hands. I could call on someone and have them answer the question from their experience, and tie it in as an introduction to the topic. Then I would go into the informational part of the class.

I noticed that when I was able to try this out in my first class, it also alerted the audience that they might be called on, and it had them paying more attention than usual to the information. They were alert and engaged, and that felt really good.

So I had an introduction in the form of audience participation. This would become a lead-in to the five key points, or benefits, of my smoothie. Then I would make the smoothie, talk about the ingredients and equipment I was using, and pass out samples. The last part I needed to create was my sales pitch, where I would invite them to talk to me for free, or to a class I had scheduled on the calendar for a few weeks out.

The segue from the information to the sales pitch was anxiety-provoking. I hated sales; it felt so uncomfortable to ask someone to pay me for what I loved to do and share. I had previously had other sales conversations, and they hadn't gone well. So how was I going to seamlessly transition from a positive content experience to asking participants to take the next step with me into a paid class or program? I decided to return to the questions, poll the audience for their experience, and make it relevant to what I did outside of the lecture. Once I changed the focus of the sales from me asking for something and made it relevant to their experience, it ended up being easy to ask if they wanted more. When I did this, I got a lot of interested people asking what was next and what was possible because it spoke to their interests and lifestyle, not just mine.

Getting curious about other people and what they really want in their lives is a powerful way to tie my work into how I can be of use. I authentically want to be of service in other people's lives. There is nothing more satisfying than being of support to someone else and helping them achieve their goals and dreams. When that happens, everyone wins! This also comes in handy when you are networking and finding it hard to explain what exactly you do, especially when your services are varied and don't always make sense as a complete thought. We will go into more detail on this later on.

Let's break my story down, and put it in perspective for your message and business:

What do you love to talk about? Choose a topic that's relevant to the services you offer. I was a chef and health coach at the time, working on getting healthy and making clean food taste great. I wanted to share the taste and benefits of my smoothie with others. I was offering cooking classes and health coaching. So sharing all the things I love in one lecture, by making this smoothie, made sense to me as a way for my audience to experience my style and the kind of work I do with clients.

Talk to a friend that has an interest in your topic. How can you educate your audience in five key points? What are things you can talk about to support your message and show the audience the benefits of this education and information?

I talked about the ingredients, their health benefits, how to make the smoothie, what equipment was needed, and why smoothies are good for you.

Create questions to poll the audience with that could tie into your topic. I figured out my questions to alert and engage the people who attended so I could take some of the attention off myself and settle into the class. I asked, "Who here has smoothies during the day?" When people raised their hands, I called on someone and asked them what their favorite combinations were. This got the audience thinking about food and flavors they like.

They also knew I had no fear about calling on them to participate, and this perked everyone up and got them paying closer attention. I then led into my topic by stating, "This is what we will be talking about today, my favorite smoothie recipe, the importance of having smoothies in your diet, and how to make them. Then we will taste what we make and have time for questions. Sound good? Let's begin."

What are your talking points? I then went into my five key points. If at any point in time I felt stuck or nervous I asked the audience another question about their experience or I asked if anyone had any questions. Then I went on to the next key point. The last part of the class was tasting the smoothie. It was at this point I could ask them to share of the smoothie and the class.

When you come to the end of your key points, ask a final question about their experience of the class. It is time to make your offer for the next steps they can take with you. This is the sales part of the class, and it makes many people nervous. I would ask, "Tell me something you are taking away from this class." After I took a few comments, I could tie this important comment into the conversation: "This is the way I work with my clients. If you enjoyed the class and the smoothie and want to learn more about how to have healthier, good-tasting food in your life that is quick and easy to make, I am having a class soon where you will learn 10 recipes to start with."

I listened and commented on their experience, their delight with the smoothie, and whatever else they learned from the lecture. Think about what you are offering. How can you invite them to go further with you, and what benefit will they get by doing so? Then give them an incentive to sign up on the spot. I would offer a discount or gift for coming to the class and signing up for the next offering. You want them to have perceived value. They already had a great experience with you. Now they can have that again in a bigger way, not to mention being rewarded for showing up to your free class.

Last, do not forget to get the participants' names and email addresses. Have a clipboard and a sign-in sheet. They all need to sign at the beginning of the class so that you can send a thank you email and make your offer again. Sometimes people get shy or they don't want to make a commitment on the spot, so the follow-up is very important to get a few people signed into your next offer after they have integrated their experience of you.

I find that many of the above tips also help ease an introduction to someone new. The question, "What do you do?" is often a formality, and yet it is also an opportunity to give the other person a positive impression of who you are and how you work with your clients. This used to be something that made me feel so uncomfortable or self-conscious, talking about myself. So I turned the traditional way we introduce ourselves around and into an experience where I could get very curious about the other person.

I had a lot of different things going on in my business. Because I wore so many hats, trying to put what I did into one sentence actually confused people. To say I was a chef or a health coach oversimplified the experience a client would have with me, and if I started naming everything else I might do with them, they would get overwhelmed. There was nothing intriguing for them to get curious about and ask me further questions. I looked at this inquiry as an opportunity. If we had already been talking and they told me something about themselves, I could use this information to ask them something. Otherwise I would say, "I'll answer that in a minute. I am curious about you." I might ask them about their health or their lifestyle. They would talk further about the topic I was asking about, and I could then relate it to what I do in a general way. For example, if they wanted to learn how to eat healthier but the food had to taste a certain way, I would put my focus on that.

I really like putting it like this: "So this is exactly what I do. I work as a coach with clients who have similar issues or lifestyles as you just shared with me, and we create a path for them to have more of what they want." I know that sounds very generic. I use specific examples from what they shared. What I am accomplishing here is showing them how I can be of benefit in a single area they are working on in their lives. Speaking to the benefits of what the other person can expect to experience with you in the way you introduce yourself is very powerful. So in this case I would say, "That's exactly what I do. The clients

I work with are similar to you in that they want to eat healthier, but they don't want to compromise on taste. They also want the preparation to be quick and easy. I work with my clients in the kitchen on recipes, and out of the kitchen talking about what works for them and what doesn't, so we can make easy, incremental changes over time to create lasting improvements to their health." And then I get completely silent, let them process what I just said, and listen for their feedback. In general, there is one of three responses: curiosity, resistance, or excitement.

In the case of curiosity and excitement you can make an offer. As for resistance, you can explore that with the client by getting curious what is coming up for them, or you can let them know the offer is available if they are ready at a later date, they may even send you a referral. There are going to be people who challenge you with their resistance, and if that does not feel like someone you want to work with then take the conversation in a different direction altogether, or thank them for listening and walk away. Many of my coach clients offer people a free consultation session in which they can look more closely at the issues, and both sides can decide if it will be a good fit. This is a good offer for a quick introductory conversation with someone. You can go a step further to establish trust later on.

One thing I *never* do is answer the price question. I tell them that I offer many ways of working together and that we can talk about that further in the consultation. Each person needs different things, so it wouldn't be in either of our best interests to go rattling off prices without having a discussion and seeing if we are a good fit to work together. People, in general, assume perceived value. But the value is their experience with you, not in the dollar price. When people have a good experience and feel they will benefit from working with you, then cost becomes less important.

As with the class, remember to get their information or business card in order to follow up or keep in touch with other offers in the future, because you never know when someone will want to talk with you later on.

As an introvert, I felt I lacked the skills to share what I do in a compelling way. It was important for me to find a way to take the attention off myself, and, lucky for me, people really like when you want to listen to what they have to say and how you can be of benefit to them. Once I figured out how to shape my conversations in a way to get curious about other people, it became easy to tie in what I do with what they were sharing with me. Even if they didn't want to go further than our conversation, I felt I left them feeling heard and engaged, so their experience with me was always a good one.

CHAPTER 6
Confidently Asking for What You're Worth

"Anxiety is fear with negative anticipation. Excitement is fear with positive anticipation. You control which one you see."

MASTIN KIPP

Now we are ready to get out into the world and start talking to people about what we do. For some this will be anxiety-provoking, and for others it will feel exhilarating. In either case, this is where you might come up with some resistance disguised in the form of confusion around how to talk to others about what you do in an engaging way. This usually shows up when someone asks you, "What is it that you do, exactly?"

Most coaches have many modalities they like to incorporate into their business. But when they try to explain this to other people, they feel like it's just not being understood or heard. Many times, trying to explain each modality and how you use them has the other person looking like a deer in the headlights with paralyzed confusion, or glazing over and losing interest in what you are saying. The bottom line is, as a service-based business person, you will need to introduce yourself in a way that is of benefit to the person you are speaking to. Gone are the days where you can just blurt out a job title, and the person will just know what that is. At least it was for Danielle, who you met briefly in Chapter 3.

Danielle followed her heart in college and double majored in psychology and fine art. She entered the job market after graduation while earning her Masters of Fine Arts in art therapy, and eventually made her way over to join her parents in their family retail business. Even though her family job was a 24/7 career, she had free time to study and participate in less traditional things such as health and wellness, allergy elimination (NAET), astrology, essential oils, crystals, and holistic pet health. She gravitated toward metaphysical modalities, as she felt called to make this a part of her life improvement process. She knew in her heart that she could be of service in this way because she always brought these practices into her conversations with others when they expressed dissatisfaction in their lives. The friends and family members who heeded her advice always felt better when they tried her suggestions. Danielle felt deeply grateful and satisfied that she could teach and support others with the things she loved that had worked in her life.

Danielle started a side business doing some life coaching and teaching classes. She had a certificate in holistic health coaching, but did not feel like she wanted to be limited to only health. She called herself a life improvement consultant. This general title could represent all the modalities she offered as well as the ones she might offer in the future. The problem with this title was that it wasn't clear to others exactly what she did, and so people did not seem interested when she shared what she did using only her title.

Danielle came to me to work on clarifying her message, explaining what she did in a way that would attract new clients, creating programs and packages, and learning to ask for the money she was worth for her expert knowledge. We talked about her modalities and her passion for working with others. Like many life coaches, her interests came from her history and personal experience of healing herself. She believed that a three-tiered approach of mind, body, and spirit was the way to heal for lasting results, and she worked in this fashion with all her clients. Danielle felt confident about her offerings and just wanted to feel understood in an impactful way when she spoke to people.

We identified together that the entry into winning someone's trust is in the first introduction of who you are, what you offer, and how you work with clients. It was here that she needed to construct a way of introducing herself so she could allow others to experience her and understand the benefits they might expect in working with her. We devised a formula that bypassed the question, "What do you do?" and instead answered the question, "What can you do for me?"

Step 1: Describe what you do in addition to stating your title

I am a life improvement consultant, which means...

Defining your chosen title by describing the benefits someone can expect from working with you will create an experience for them in which they can get a glimpse of who you are and how it will benefit them to listen further.

Step 2: How do you work with clients?

I work with my clients by...

Sometimes you will be asked this question separately. Other times it can be an extension of your response to the first question, if you feel you have the other person's interest. There is a fine line here, so make sure you are really paying attention to the other person as this conversation is for their benefit.

You genuinely want to support people who could use your help, not overwhelm someone with sales they aren't interested in.

Step 3: Use something they've shared with you to create an experience for them.

So I'll give you an example of what I mean. You shared with me that you...

Bring something to their attention that they mentioned to you and where you feel your service can be of use. This shows the other person that you are a good listener, and means they will feel excited that your attention was on what they were saying. Use this piece of information to describe how you might work with them using what you practice, and describe what benefits they could expect as a result. An alternative here would be to use a client story or a friend story where you can easily and quickly show the problem and what the result was after that person worked with you.

Step 4: Make the connection

The way I would work with you is...

By talking with the person in this way, you've created a journey for them to understand what it is you do and personally give them an example of something that they could expect by working with you. You've made it personal, which engages their interest and helps them more clearly understand how they can benefit from working with you.

Step 5: Make a benign offer

This is the point where you could show even more interest in them, and ask some additional questions about their situation. You'll then ask, "Would you be interested in learning more?" At this point, you can offer an invitation to an entry level or free opportunity in which they can experience you further. Consider a free, 20-minute exploratory call or a free one-hour session where you can talk all about them and see if you both are a good fit to work together.

Step 6: Put it on the calendar and get their information

This is the most important step to transitioning into a possible sale. If you walk away without something on the calendar, your chance of converting them into a client goes down significantly. Ask them to take out their calendar and give you a time in the coming week when it would be good to reconnect. Get their information so you can send a reminder and follow up.

When Danielle used this new method of introducing herself, she was overwhelmed by the response. Almost everyone wanted to know more, which meant she now had to work on her boundaries! Instead of coaching people on the spot, she needed to work on pointing out that this was what her free session was for: to get deeper into personal issues so she could really devote all her attention to that person. When she answered in this way, the other person felt seen and respected – and in turn respected Danielle's space in the immediate moment. Her conversion rate from initial introduction to free session sky-rocketed.

When you have your free conversation, you have an opportunity to invite the person to take the next step with you. Although we will not go over how to have that conversation with a prospective client in this book, what's important is to be very clear about what you are offering. Many coaches get overwhelmed by trying to figure which of their modalities is the right service to offer a prospective client. The key is to figure out the story of how all your services can fit together and offer them as a package.

Remember Jessica from Chapter 3? Jessica is a health coach and has a certification in Nutrition Response Testing. She has been successful in her holistic business and has aligned herself with a doctor who refers his patients to her. She helps clients understand their food allergies, and then works with them in a six-month health coaching program to support them in their lifestyle and food changes. This has them feeling confident and accountable to making good changes and feeling great. In her personal life, Jessica practices reiki and has found that she maintains life balance by clearing her energy. She found herself discussing reiki with her friends, and they were a little skeptical, but intrigued to try it out. After a session, Jessica's friends commented on the subtle shifts they were feeling and seeing in their lives. Jessica was delighted and wanted to offer reiki to her clients, but she felt uncomfortable about how she would incorporate an energetic practice into her current offerings.

When Jessica explained to me her dilemma I could see how she was uncomfortable explaining reiki to patients. Her confidence to sell energy healing was low because she felt there were no tangible results like she achieved with her other services, and she worried that her patients would feel like she was selling them snake oil. She wasn't willing to risk being judged for offering a service she knew in her heart was helpful, but might be seen as unbelievable. She had held off reviewing her package structure and pricing due to this ambivalence.

As we discussed, the way she offers clients her packages at the end of her free session, it occurred to me that if she had a story she could tell, she wouldn't feel like she was selling just reiki. Holistic means seeing the parts of something as intimately interconnected and explicable only by reference to the whole. In this case, the parts of the whole are mind, body, *and* spirit, whereas Jessica had only been offering the mind and body parts of her whole picture. When I asked her how she felt about that, she lit up. There was now a way to create her top package offering that would heal her patients on both the more observable and the more subtle levels, which would result in a sense of well-being that her patients would not get from a regular dietician or medical doctor.

Jessica practiced offering this mind, body, spirit package that now included an initial NRT session, followed by six months of accountability health coaching and three reiki sessions. Jessica felt confident and clear about her offerings, and this shone through with every patient she offered the package to. She felt so excited about offering reiki that she revisited her current patients' packages with them and offered them a discounted rate that included reiki sessions. Almost all of them were on board. Jessica really believed in everything she could offer. As soon as she was clear on how to offer it, her business soared.

The last part of the sales process – meeting the prospective client, having a free session with them, and making them an offer to work with you – is asking for money. Everyone has a hard time with money in some way or another. As coaches, we deserve to earn what we feel we are worth. We need to get really clear that what we have to offer is amazing and of benefit for the type of people we want to work with. Until you are ready to work through the beliefs you have around money and how they are keeping you from being successful, you will not be able to ask for what you are worth.

Rachel wasn't confident about her pricing. She was excited about her services and offerings. She knew that her high-end package offer was a closet clean-out, a six-hour shopping trip, and a follow-up to make outfits of the new items and the old clothes the client chose to keep. She also offered her eBay account to the client if they wanted to sell designer items to make back some of their money. She offered variations of these services depending on how her exploratory conversation went with the client.

She asked me what I thought she should charge. The first thing I suggested was that she do some research and see what other professionals in her industry were offering and charging. Rachel also needed to consider what she would like to make for an hour of her time. Once she had these two pieces of information, we could then talk about prices she felt comfortable asking for.

The conversation started with a lot of resistance around charging as much as the other professionals in her field. She didn't feel she had enough experience to charge the going rates of someone who had been doing it a long time. I could feel she was underselling herself, so we broke down her package into how many hours she would devote to a client and all the prep work that would be involved. Her package came to around 24 hours she would spend with a client that bought into all her service offerings. When she saw exactly how many hours she would be spending on one client, she started to get clear on how much she would want to make per hour. The prices she had been thinking of had her making about $30 an hour, while the other professionals in her industry were making $150 an hour. Breaking your packages down in this way can be one way to really see the value of what you are offering and where you might be shortchanging yourself. This also showed Rachel how much each service would cost, in terms of time, if she offered them a la carte.

Rachel's goal was to sell packages, so she increased the prices of the a la carte options so that there would be a perceived value in the package price. This also ensured that if a client were to pick one service only, Rachel would get paid what her expertise was worth for her time. She could then decide later on whether she wanted to extend a reduced rate for additional a la carte options with repeat clients.

Rachel was clear on her worth, and she felt good about her packages and prices. Now she had to go practice inviting clients into her services and stating the cost.

Rachel was anxiety-ridden during her first free consultation. Nevertheless, she listened to her client's concerns and goals, and felt comfortable that she had the solution. She confidently answered all the client's questions about how a shopping package might look by using benefit statements and painting a picture of how they would work together to find the client's signature style. As she described each of her a la carte services, she spoke to the benefits and of what the client could expect. The picture was painted, and the client was ready to pay.

"How much is your full package?" asked the client. Rachel felt a lump in her throat. Her voice got higher and higher, as if she were asking a question, when she stated the price. She had lost all confidence and started stammering to explain the service again. She felt that her explanations were like nails on a chalkboard. If she could just pause, take a breath, and compose herself, she could get through asking for the sale.

The client started to explain that she would have to talk to her husband about the cost. Rachel knew that was just an excuse to get off the phone, so she took a deep breath, found her previous strong and enthusiastic tone, and told the client, "I'm confident you're going to be thrilled with your signature style. So I'd like to offer you a reduced package price where you get all the services I mentioned all together at a discount." This reengaged the client, and Rachel started to explain the savings. As long as Rachel could maintain her tone in a conversation as she transitioned from the benefits part of the conversation to the part where she had to discuss money, the client felt supported and confident. From that day on, her client onboarding rate tripled.

Many of my clients have the same confidence issues I had. Being a creative professional isn't a straight forward and traditional way to do business. Being a creative introvert and not succeeding in the traditional ways of doing business, I had to find ways to explain what I had created and how it could be of benefit to whoever I was talking to. I found that by getting curious about the other person, I had some material to create a story for them – and it was a relief to have the attention off myself. What ended up happening was that they felt heard. It is such a gift to feel deeply listened to and truly seen, and that was a byproduct of getting the attention off of myself and onto them. It turned a boring answer into an experience I could share with them. Even if they never became my client, we both walked away from the interaction feeling engaged.

The clients who wanted to spend more time with me in a free session were the ones I also wanted to talk more with. This gave me an opportunity to get to know them at a deeper level. When I spoke to a perspective client, I could get a glimpse of their inner world and the places where they were lacking in confidence. I could feel where they needed the most attention. It was these places that got brought out and loved in the session with me.

I had a hard time asking for money in the beginning, because I was afraid to be rejected. I was afraid that my expertise and desire to be of service to others wouldn't be appreciated or seen. There were some cases in the beginning when prospective clients challenged me, and I didn't know how to react. The more I tried to prove my knowledge to them, the further I felt them drifting into saying no to my offer. I needed a reality check that what I was offering was a gift and that many people would benefit, the way I felt when I taught my first smoothie class. When I could tap into that place of flow and confidence, not pausing out of insecurity from expecting a the client to say no, I observed how we both flowed into a yes. Maintaining my confidence through the whole session had the client feeling a sense of security that I could help and support them in their goals. A yes from a client felt like a new exciting journey was about to begin. Now we could get to the fun stuff.

CHAPTER 7
Pitfalls and Obstacles

"If you don't encounter setbacks in
your career, if you don't have doubts
and disappointments, let me tell you,
you're not dreaming big enough."

MICHAEL BLOOMBERG

At this point, you have taken a deep dive into yourself
and what you have to offer the world. You have faced
your fears and let go of what is longer serving
you. You feel a sense of freedom and have given
yourself permission to finally do the thing you love.

You have identified what the new you looks like and have started to practice and gain confidence in being an expert. You know that what you have to offer is special and needed, and the type of people you like to work with are abundant. Your prices and services are all set for this group of people, and you've gotten out into the world and started talking about what you do and how it is of benefit for others. You're working out the kinks and it feels good. You're both excited and nervous about the way you're increasingly in sync with yourself, your message, and your connection with others. But even though you are the expert you have come to be and your services are valuable to many, even though you're willing to do what it takes to consciously step further into this new you, there will still be places where you will fail.

One of the ways entrepreneurs fail is by going back to what they knew because it is more comfortable then growing into the unknown. They don't have the proper support set up in their everyday life, or the people to root their success to keep them moving forward. It isn't because these people don't believe in you, it is because they want you to be secure and safe. Starting up your own business has risk to it, but the bigger risk is in not forging ahead and doing what it takes to be successful no matter what. It's not meant to be easy. If it were, it would be called play and not work. The good news is our hard work can often feel like play when we are doing what we love. Don't take no for an answer. Your own no should not be acceptable, but it will sometimes show up in such tricky ways that you don't realize you're saying no. The reasons for your no will feel very valid, but may get you feeling stuck. You might even abandon what you've worked so hard to create.

I have given you a comprehensive guide to go inside yourself and come back out as an authentic and confident version of you. If you have followed these steps and done the work, there will still be ways you will sabotage, betray, and abandon yourself. I know first-hand because in the last 15 years I have showed up to do my work, been open to dropping what no longer serves me, and taken on new layers of who I am meant to be and how I am meant to work with others. Yet I still have gotten in my own way time and again. I've even quit my projects and convinced myself I was the victim instead of the cause of not moving forward. Even now, as I share this, it feels like a vulnerable place to admit that I have failed myself, even when the thing I wanted most was to be successful by serving others in the way I am meant to by staying open to that which is always evolving. The one thing that kept me moving forward and working through those tough times when I couldn't see what I was doing to myself was being accountable to someone and working with a coach. The coaches I have worked with over the years have all had their own specialties and styles, but what they all had in common was a way to show me where I was getting stuck, to help me face my fears, and to support me in a new strategy to get to my next level.

Here are a few examples of how you can get in your own way.

I don't want to get out and be seen

Rachel was growing her business and becoming popular in her community of moms. She had consistent work and repeat clients, but didn't feel like her efforts were paying off in a big enough way. She felt the pressure to quickly make more money because she wanted to buy a house for her growing family and wanted her work to support the kind of lifestyle she wanted after only one year of growing her business.

Her belief was that people weren't interested in her service. There was plenty of evidence that this wasn't true. She was starting to get requests to talk to mom groups about trends and styles. There were women who were going back to work and looking for new wardrobes that would fit their bodies properly after having babies. There were women who had lost weight and wanted to update their look. Not only were pregnant moms looking for style, their friends who were not pregnant were inquiring of Rachel's services and hiring her as well.

Rachel felt that she spent a lot of time on her digital marketing efforts and her reach wasn't what she had dreamed of. The truth was that Rachel was hiding behind her stagnant newsletter and limited Facebook business page as an excuse to stop putting in more visible effort. She didn't feel comfortable getting out and being seen by groups of women that sincerely wanted style advice. Rachel knew she was a powerhouse one-on-one, but in order to take her business to the next level she would have to get in front of more people to grow her business, and this freaked her out. Slowly she started to withdraw from her work and complain that people weren't interested. Instead of facing her fears and growing in the place that scared her by asking for help or support in public speaking and online presence, she decided to quit personal fashion and take courses in another profession. It might or might not give her the compensation she was looking for, but she wouldn't have to face those uncomfortable places her fashion business was asking her to look at and grow. She got to the point where she would rather have started all over in something else instead of doing the things she loved since she was a girl, because it was too confronting and she couldn't figure out by herself how to move it forward.

I'm not worth it

Jessica got to a place in her business that was comfortable. She had two doctors referring clients to her for NRT and health coaching. She was very happy with how she was working with those clients and with the progress they were making. She had not raised her prices in a few years; the thought of asking for more was confronting. She didn't even have a sense of what her services were worth because she had established her initial pricing based on what one of the doctors thought she should charge when she was a new practitioner. Jessica called on some other NRT professionals to research their pricing and found out they were, on average, charging three times the amount she was for one session. She was shocked by the fact that they were getting paying clients with such high prices. She felt sad that she had underpriced herself for so long, but the thought of asking for that much money was terrifying because she felt she would lose all her current clients. Even though she now knew she had more earning potential, she convinced herself that she was happy enough to keep her prices where they were. But day after day, she grew resentful about all the potential income she could be making. Jessica became miserable. She knew she had to stretch herself in this area and find a way to increase her prices without losing her clients, but how?

Jessica asked me for help. We identified her issues with money and self-worth. She had a story from her childhood experience that she should just take what was given to her and not ask for any more. When she identified this story, she was able to work with it and start to make a plan to talk to her current clients about her revised rates. The first thing we looked at was how much her services were worth per hour. She knew she wanted to make $150 per hour, but when we broke down her hours of work with each client in their current package prices, she realized she was making $35 an hour. She had never thought of her time in this way. It suddenly made sense why she was grossly underpaid for her valuable service that was healing so many people.

Once she arrived at this conclusion, Jessica was then able to go back and revise her packages and prices. When it came time to talk to her clients, she could explain that when their package expired, she was going to raise her service prices and would give them a reduced rate from the new package price because they were her current clients. She felt really great about this offer and even contacted clients she had worked with in the past to invite them back into her offerings with this same reduced-rate package. Jessica got clear and wise about the way she was undervaluing herself and her services. Instead of sitting in her resentment, she found a way to have what she needed to continue to support herself and further ignite her passion in the way she was working with her clients. She thought she was happy and satisfied in the work she was doing, but really, she was hiding behind the comfort of what she had created a few years back. Refreshing and updating your services is important and necessary, but it isn't always easy to look at and change by yourself.

I don't know enough

Danielle loved taking classes and learning new things. She had been studying astrology both in person and online for eight years. Almost every conversation she had involved astrology; she followed the transits every day and could speak knowledgeably to anyone about their chart and what they were going through at the present time. Her friends and family took comfort in this information, as did Danielle with her personal astrologers.

Her astrologer, Anne, had become a close friend over the years, and one day at lunch Anne told

Danielle it was time to get certified and start doing professional readings. Danielle was nervous about this idea. She felt that although there was so much she understood, there was still so much to learn. She found herself making excuses to Anne about why she didn't think this was a good idea. She didn't want to take the certification test because it might prove her fear that she wasn't proficient enough to read a chart. Or she could take the certification test, be proven wrong, and find that she knew everything necessary to start doing readings. Then she would feel able to move forward and ask for money for the readings she liked giving for free.

Often, doing what we love doesn't feel like work; we want to be of support to others and give away our advice for free. Danielle liked to feel of use and inspiration and didn't want to feel the pressure of having to know everything right away in order to give a good reading. This was a pattern with Danielle. She had studied so many modalities that were near and dear to her, but offering them as a service made her feel that she didn't know enough to be an expert.

Anne talked to Danielle about how she herself had started with basic readings for a long time until she felt more confident to add in more interpretive astrology. The story and examples that Anne shared with Danielle allowed her to start considering how she might do a basic reading at a reduced price. Danielle went to work in a crystal shop shortly after this conversation with Anne. She found herself in many astrology conversations with the customers, and some of them asked if she did readings. She offered them a basic reading for $30. Their positive reactions made her more comfortable with what she was doing. She started to feel that she indeed did know enough and started to increase her rate over time.

It is difficult to accept being an expert in the area you know and love. With practice and by starting at a pace that works for you, you can slowly see that what you are offering is of tremendous value to another in their awareness and growth. What makes you an expert is that you took the time to learn these things and can teach them or practice them with someone who will benefit from your knowledge.

I am not ready to grow/I don't want to do all the jobs required to expand my business

When I graduated from IIN, I was on top of the world. Every morning I would wake up and intuitively know what project was on tap for that day. My weeks were eagerly spent finding ways to connect with a larger audience and being of use to attract clients. In the first year of my health coaching business, I soared. I was out in the community every day. But by the end of the year, I was feeling a bit over extended and retreated to take stock of where my efforts had been successful, in order to put more attention on those efforts and make room for new projects. I immediately got offered the opportunity to coach the current students at IIN. I felt even more in flow and of use as they realized their dreams and got clear on their business offerings. It was a team effort. As a result, after the year was over I decided to reinvent my business to include business development coaching for new coaches.

I hired a business coach to help me pivot into this new target and, even with my coach's support, I got overwhelmed by the idea that I needed to start my marketing efforts over to attract the new target market. I made up in my mind the story that marketing was not my area of expertise. I became the victim to marketing my business, and this gave me the excuse I needed to get smaller and go back to focusing on health coaching instead of pushing forward and expanding into what I really wanted, which was to help new coaches gain their confidence and voice in their new endeavors.

I was shrinking away from the very thing I wanted to support others in becoming. I thought I needed marketing coaching, and as a result I spent thousands of dollars gaining that knowledge and then did nothing with it. It wasn't that I needed more skills, it was that I needed to look at myself and the fact that I didn't want to do the marketing, so I was sabotaging my efforts and my ability to go after my dreams. For a very long time I couldn't see what I was doing to myself. I blamed myself for being a failure, even though I knew and had proved that I could be successful the previous year.

I don't want this to happen to you. It's important to have an accountability partner or a coach that can show you the places where you are not showing up for yourself and give you the tools to work through these places and move forward into flow.

I am that coach! Working with me, you will get a no-nonsense approach to stepping through your blocks so you can keep moving forward. I take a loving stand for all my clients to step into their confidence over and over in all the uncomfortable ways that pop up, so they can have what they want. I needed that back then, and now I can identify when to ask for accountability and help to get through a rough spot so I can step back into the entrepreneur I know I am and be of support to my clients and my purpose. I will teach you how to identify when and how you get blocked, so you won't be victimized by this as I was. I am going to be your ultimate partner in accountability so you can continue to soar and have the purposeful career you want, the one that led you to this book in the first place.

CONCLUSION

You are cordially invited...

To live your best life by creating the best version of your authentic self. Find your voice confidently, and do the work you are meant to do using your creative talents and message. Create a life based on the way you are the most productive, and step away from the traditional ways of doing business.

I find creative professionals and coaches to be the most interesting people to work with because they have so much passion. It's fascinating to see how people with so much passion can self-sabotage. They allow their crossed wires and doubt to get in the way of their success. Creative types of people have the most to offer this world. Their work comes from a place so deep down they often don't realize what a gift it is to share it. It is something they are excited about every day, so sharing it just feels normal.

This gift is usually so highly personal to the story of who they are that it may be hard to describe in a compelling way or feel edgy to bring out, because it doesn't usually mesh with the traditional work roles of the outside world. There may be a lot of shame associated with wanting to bring your passion projects into the world because of the "shoulds" of society that tell us there's only one way to succeed or one way of doing business.

I am here to tell you that you can have it the way that suits you best. The way that optimizes your productivity, the way that brings out your message and offerings. It will all come from a place of deep confidence that your interests and passions are very much needed. I am going to help you bring it out in a way that feels authentic and comes from the core of your being. That may sound deep and ethereal, but it is true. I am going to guide you in a way so that you can fully come into the person you are meant to be and offer your passionate creative and deeply supportive side to others in a way where you feel safe and natural, fully expressing what excites you in a way that benefits others.

How do I know this is possible? This is a journey I have been on for the last 15 years. I have lived with the insecurities and the "I don't knows." I have come to the other side, and know that what I have to say and what I have to offer my clients is deeply important and healing to their lives.

There were times I took this gift for granted or didn't want to see that it was necessary to bring it out. As a deep introvert, I realized that what I have to share is bigger than who I am as a person. I desperately needed a way to find my voice in a way that reflected who I truly am. It had to feel comfortable, or I would retreat and return to the traditional way of doing things. Then I'd have to hear "I told you so" from all those people who couldn't see me for who I am and were trying to keep me safe by asking me to stay small.

So, with this book, I encourage you to come out in the best way. I invite you to discover how to find your voice through your creativity, passion, and gifts in a way that feels like you're just having lunch and a wonderful conversation with your best friend.

It's simple if you do the work and you're ready to really see yourself and make some changes. Most importantly, you're ready to own who you really are, despite that the outside world tells you what you should be. Are you ready? I am so excited for us to do this together ... here we go!

ACKNOWLEDGEMENTS

Dana, you are my favorite person on the planet, and I thank you for always seeing me and calling me out to be the best version of myself. I am grateful to have a best friend and sister all wrapped in one dynamite package. Through you I feel understood, supported, unconditionally loved, and funny. Our relationship is one of great caring and compassion.

I give thanks to my spirit guides and teachers for guiding me in my life lessons and going on this journey with me from where I am now to who I am to become. My friend, teacher, guide, and astrologer, Anne Ortelee, entered my life in 2008 during a spiritual awakening when my life started to exquisitely fall away and allow for the new.

Anne, it has been an exciting and bumpy ride, and there were times I knew that had it not been for your wisdom, guidance, support, and loving, no-nonsense approach, I might not be on the planet today. You have guided me in a way that brings me patience and understanding of myself and the world around me to be able to truly embrace my heart through my chart. I am truly blessed.

To the Morgan James Publishing team: Special thanks to David Hancock, CEO & Founder for believing in me and my message. To my Author Relations Manager, Gayle West, thanks for making the process seamless and easy. Many more thanks to everyone else, but especially Jim Howard, Bethany Marshall, and Nickcole Watkins.

ABOUT THE AUTHOR

Stacey Weckstein, founder of Radiant Mind and Body LLC, helps new coaches and creative entrepreneurs find their inner voice so that they have the confidence to bring their authentic selves out into the world.

Stacey's keen sense of what works is backed by a thorough education in psychology, health, nutrition, training, and management. She is a certified health counselor and has trained at the Institute for Integrative Nutrition in New York (accredited by Columbia Teachers College).

She holds a bachelor's degree in psychology from Boston University, giving her a deep understanding of the motivations behind food, career, and lifestyle choices. She spent a decade in management with some of the most successful food businesses in the country.

Stacey has helped businesses achieve dramatic improvements in their organization and focus – in turn, making their businesses more profitable. Clients who seek Stacey's guidance are ready to get real and get wise, both in terms of health and business goals. She helps coaches quickly recognize easy-to-integrate strategies that suit their work style and help eliminate confusion about next steps, which in turn boosts their confidence and their bottom line.

Stacey is a classically trained culinary chef from Johnson & Wales University and a certified raw foods chef, a certified yoga instructor, reiki master, an iRest facilitator.

Website: www.MagnifyYourPurpose.com

THANK YOU

Thank you for reading *Magnify Your Purpose: An Introverts Guide to Creating a Coaching Business that Reflects Who You Are.*

I sincerely hope this book has provided you with the insight and encouragement to build the coaching business that truly represents who you are and has you ready to come out of your shell and reach those clients who truly need you.

In order to help you move to your next level, I have created a FREE class for you entitled, "Three Mistakes New Coaches Make While Creating Their Signature Talk." This will help you avoid the most common missteps new coaches make when coming up with their signature message to attract clients.

Please visit my website, <u>www.MagnifyYourPurpose.com</u>, to download your free copy.

I wish you all the best.

Stacey Weckstein

Morgan James
Speakers Group

↗ www.TheMorganJamesSpeakersGroup.com

We connect Morgan James published
authors with live and online events
and audiences who will benefit
from their expertise.

Morgan James makes all of our titles available
through the Library for All Charity Organization.

www.LibraryForAll.org